ORCA
KILLER WHALE

SELENA DALE

ORCA
KILLER WHALES

Selena Dale

FREE GIFTS!

Just to say thank you for purchasing this book, I want to give you some free gifts.

Collect your free gifts here:

www.selenadale.com/get-your-free-gifts

Table of Contents

Introduction

Introduction

Orca Killer Whales are huge sea animals many of which are as big as a school bus! Now that's big!

So what does something that big eat?
Where does this amazing animal live?
Why are they called killer whales?
Why is it a mammal and not a fish?
What exactly is a mammal?

These questions and many more are answered in this fun book where you will get a closer look at the life of the Orca – Killer Whale.

Enjoy learning about these sea mammals by reading the chapter and then going through the fun questions and answers quiz.

Click on the images if you want to enlarge them.

1. BASICS - WHAT IS THE ORCA?

Two Orcas coming up for air

The Orca is one of the world's most powerful predators. This huge predator of the oceans is known by a number of names.

Its original name is Orcinus orca, but it is also referred to as the Orca whale, Orca killer whale and less commonly as the blackfish.

Orcas have large and very long, rounded bodies. A large part of their body is black with white sections on the underside and near their eyes.

They have left and right flippers as well as a large dorsal fin right in the middle of their backs.

These beautiful animals are highly social and travel in groups which are called Pods. These family Pod groups can have up to 40 individuals all swimming and hunting together.

Due to the massive size and powerful strength. Orcas are among the fastest marine mammals. They can reach speeds of up to 35mph.
Now that is some pretty fast swimming!

Orcas are mammals.

What Are Mammals?

- Mammals breathe air with lungs.

- Mammals are warm-blooded. This means their core temperature stays the same regardless of how cold or warm its surroundings are.

- Mammals nurse their young with milk.

- Mammals have hair at some stage in their development...but I don't mean hair on their heads like humans!

It is not officially known how many Orcas live in our oceans worldwide but a rough estimate would be around 50,000. Now that may sound like a lot, but when you consider the size of our oceans it really isn't that many.

Just another dive before bedtime

Size: Male orcas can grow up to 23 feet long. Females can grow up to 21 feet.

Weight: Males weigh 7 to 10 tons, and females weigh 4 to 6 tons.

Lifespan: Orcas live 30 to 50 years in the wild.

FUN FACT:
Did you know that Orcas belong to the dolphin family?

QUIZ QUESTIONS

1. One of the names for the Orca is "Orca _____Whale" What word goes in the blank space?

2. What are the two main colors found on the Orca's body?

3. Where will you find the dorsal fin on the Orca's body?

4. What are the family groups called?

5. How fast can an Orca swim?

6. Are there any 80 year old Orcas in the sea?

QUIZ ANSWERS

1. Killer.

2. Black and white.

3. In the middle of its back.

4. Pods.

5. 35mph.

6. No. The oldest Orca can reach 50 years old.

2. HABITAT – WHERE DO THEY LIVE?

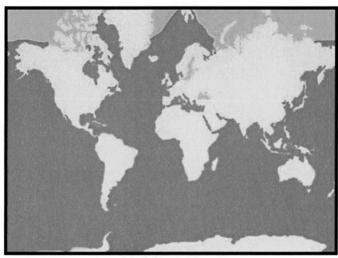

Habitat Map

Look at the map above and notice that all the orange areas are where Orca whales have been found. That is quite a big chunk of the world isn't it?

Orca whales have an enormous range which basically means they can be found in many oceans all over the world.

Generally, most of these whales are commonly found in areas of cold-water. These include places such as the Pacific Northwest, the Atlantic and the Southern Ocean.

The Killer Whale's favourite places seem to be the Arctic and the Antarctic because this is where they will find lots of food for themselves. These sea predators love to eat!

Orcas are found in both coastal waters and open ocean. They don't seem to be too fussy about where they go as long as there is food in those areas.

So, in addition to being found in colder waters, Orcas have also been found in warmer areas such as Florida, Hawaii, Australia, the Galapagos Islands, the Bahamas, New Zealand and South Africa.

Now, you won't find many of these whales in the warm temperatures but once in a while they do turn up which tells us that Orcas are not afraid to try out different waters.

FUN FACT:
"Orca" is the Latin word for the shape of a barrel or cask.

Just having some fun!

QUIZ QUESTIONS

1. Are all Orcas found in just one ocean or in many oceans?

2. Which is the Orca's favorite place to hunt for food....the Arctic, the Antarctic or both?

3. Name 2 warm climate areas that some Killer Whales have been found. Here is one example: South Africa.

4. Why do these whales prefer the cold-water areas?

QUIZ ANSWERS

1. Many oceans.

2. Both.

3. Answers can be: Florida, New Zealand, Hawaii, Australia, the Galapagos Islands, the Bahamas.

4. Cold-water areas is where they will find the most fish. Orca whales love to eat fish!

3. PHYSICAL CHARACTERISTICS

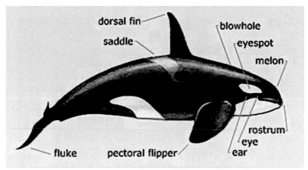

Anatomy of a Killer Whale

An adult male Killer Whale is usually larger than a female whale.

The largest male killer whale was 32 feet in length and weighed 22,000 lbs. The largest female was 28 feet and weighed 16,500 lbs. Now those where big whales! An average-size male is about 19-22 feet long while females average 16-19 feet long.

Generally, the body shape of an Orca is fairly round which happens to be a very useful shape to help the animal with energy efficiency while swimming.

Their special shape creates less drag when they propel themselves through the water. This means as they swim the water just flows around their bodies easily.

All Killer Whales are black and white, with a gray patch called a "saddle" on the back behind their dorsal fin.

Also, each whale has a unique mark behind its dorsal fin. These marks help scientists to distinguish each whale while researching.

A killer whale uses its rounded, paddle like left and right flippers to steer with the help of its tail, known as a Fluke.

Believe it or not, the whale's flipper contains five digits much like the fingers on your hand.

The flat end of the tail is called a Fluke. Actually, there are two flat sections that make up the end of the tail. Both of these Flukes are flat pads of tough tissue, completely without bone or cartilage.

The flat part of the tail is called the Fluke

The dorsal fin in the middle of its back is just the same as the two Flukes on its tail because it is also made of tough tissue and has no bone.

This dorsal fin will help stabilize the whale as it swims at high speeds, but it is not essential for the whale's balance.

As a mammal the whale has to come up for air in order to survive. In the top of its head there is a small hole called a Blowhole. The whale uses this to breathe.
These whales have only one set of teeth; they are not replaced once lost.

A killer whale does not chew its food. What it does is tear its food into smaller chunks. Their teeth are about 3 inches long!

A whale Pod group

FUN FACT:
As mammals, Killer Whales need to breathe air from the top of the ocean; they cannot breathe under water like fish.

QUIZ QUESTIONS

1. Is the female Killer Whale bigger than the male?

2. What is the general body shape of these whales?

3. What is the gray patch on its back called?

4. How does the whale steer itself in the water?

5. How many digits are in its flippers?

6. What are the flat parts of the tail called?

7. What does the whale breathe through when it comes up for air?

8. How do these whales eat their food?

QUIZ ANSWERS

1. No.

2. Round.

3. A saddle.

4. It uses its flippers.

5. A flipper has 5 digits.

6. Flukes.

7. Its Blowhole.

8. There tear chunks off their food but do not chew.

4. SEE, HEAR, TASTE AND SMELL

Orcas love to dive in and out of the water

These amazing mammals have a well-developed, acute sense of hearing.

Within each Pod the whales make a wide variety of sounds so that they can communicate with the other whales in the Pod family. Each pod has distinctive noises that its members will recognize even at a distance.

As well as having good hearing the whales also have well developed vision too. They have acute vision both in and out of water.

The eyes are located in front of and below the eye spot and the lenses are actually stronger than that of a land mammal.

The Orca's sense of touch is also quite well developed with its most sensitive area being the blowhole region and areas around the eyes and mouth.

It also looks like the whales are quite picky when it comes to choosing their food. They seem to like specific types of fish rather than any old fish that comes along.

Finally, after discovering that these whales have almost all well-developed senses we discover that they have no sense of smell. Well, I doubt having a nose would help them much under water!

More diving

FUN FACT:
A Killer whale's brain is five times larger than a human's brain. I wonder, would that make them smarter than us?

QUIZ QUESTIONS

1. How good is the Orca's hearing?

2. How do whales communicate with each other?

3. Can whales see out of water too?

4. Where are their eyes on their body?

5. Where is its most sensitive area?

6. Do Orca like to eat any old fish or are they a bit fussy?

7. How good is their sense of smell?

QUIZ ANSWERS

1. Pretty good. It is well developed.

2. They make a variety of sounds.

3. Yes, they see well out of water.

4. Their eyes are located in front of and below the eye spot.

5. The blowhole region and areas around the eyes and mouth.

6. They are fussy eaters.

7. They do not have a sense of smell.

5. SWIMMING

A mummy Orca and her baby

Orca whales are among the fastest swimming marine mammals and can swim up to 35mph for a few seconds if they are chasing prey or need to get out of trouble fast.

Most of the time they tend to leisurely cruise through the water at around 8 to 10 mph. When they swim near the surface they can stay below water for 30 seconds or less.

These whales are pretty good divers although they don't usually do much deep diving unless they are after prey. A Killer Whale can dive to at least 330 feet and on some occasions they can even dive deeper although that is not common.

While they swim the killer whale may make three or four 15-second dives. Each dive may last up to four minutes before they take another dive.
A whale will hold its breath when under water. As it swims upwards towards the surface it will open its blowhole and exhale just before it gets to the top.

Once it is at the surface it will quickly inhale air and its blowhole will close up and prepare for another dive.

Killer Whales can love too

FUN FACT:
Orcas are called "Killer Whales" because they feed on a number of other marine mammals. They do not kill people!

QUIZ QUESTIONS

1. How fast can Orcas swim?

2. How fast is their usual swimming speed?

3. Do Orcas dive really deep very often?

4. How deep can they dive?

5. What does a whale do when it goes underwater?

QUIZ ANSWERS

1. They can swim up to 35mph.

2. During a leisurely swim their speed will be around 8 to 10 mph.

3. No, they rarely dive deep.

4. They can dive to 330 feet or more.

5. It holds its breath.

6. WHAT DO KILLER WHALES EAT?

Orcas have long and sharp teeth

Even though certain varieties of whale are fussy eaters when it comes to fish, generally they are known to prey on at least 150 different species of animal.

These animals include bony fishes, sharks, squid, birds, seals, penguins and even other whales.

These whales eat up to 5% of their body weight each day. That is about 500 pounds of food. Now that is a lot of eating!

On occasions when the whale cannot catch anything in the water it will look for seals sitting on the ice above the surface. When it finds a seal it will swim up and out of the water, grab the seals right off the ice and drag it underwater.

Killer Whales usually hunt cooperatively in their pod groups. They will all work together to encircle and herd small prey before attacking.

An Orca whale trying to catch a Seal to eat

FUN FACT:
Killer whales have sharp, cone-shaped teeth that are perfect for ripping and tearing their prey.

QUIZ QUESTIONS

1. How many different species of animals do these whales eat?

2. Do these whales eat other whales too?

3. How many pounds of food do they eat each day?

4. How does a Killer Whale catch a seal?

QUIZ ANSWERS

1. They can eat 150 different species of animals.

2. Yes.

3. They average around 500 pounds of food each day.

4. It swims out of the water and then grabs the Seal.

About Selena

Selena Dale was born in United Kingdom, London and has lived there most of her life. She has a passion for writing and loves to learn new things, especially if she can share what she has learned with her two children.

Due to her varied interests and love of writing she decided to create children's books. She can now pick and choose any topic to write about while sharing what she has written with her kids.

"Young children's brains are like sponges, ready to absorb all that wonderful knowledge. A child who loves to read is a child whose imagination will be flexed like a muscle. Now that is a pretty good foundation."

Selena Dale

www.selenadale.com

Check Out My Other Books

Just go to Amazon and search for "Selena Dale Books"

OR

Got to www.selenadale.com

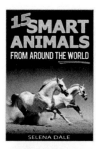

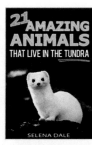

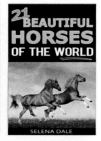

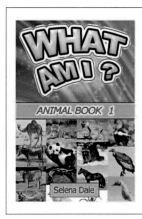 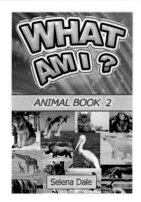 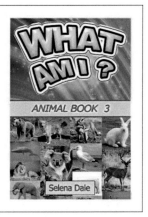

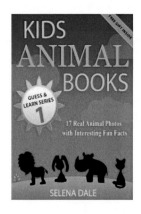  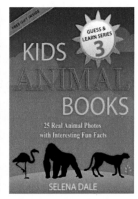

MANY MORE FUN CHILDREN'S BOOKS COMING SOON!

Made in the USA
San Bernardino, CA
28 July 2017